The Sociopathic Jesus

The Sociopathic Jesus

A Mistranslation of the Gospel of Mark

Rev. Jeff Hood

WIPF & STOCK · Eugene, Oregon

THE SOCIOPATHIC JESUS
A Mistranslation of the Gospel of Mark

Copyright © 2016 Jeff Hood. All rights reserved. Except for brief quotations in critical publications or reviews, no part of this book may be reproduced in any manner without prior written permission from the publisher. Write: Permissions, Wipf and Stock Publishers, 199 W. 8th Ave., Suite 3, Eugene, OR 97401.

Wipf & Stock
An Imprint of Wipf and Stock Publishers
199 W. 8th Ave., Suite 3
Eugene, OR 97401

www.wipfandstock.com

PAPERBACK ISBN: 978-1-5326-1247-3
HARDCOVER ISBN: 978-1-5326-1249-7

Manufactured in the U.S.A.   NOVEMBER 29, 2016

To Fred Phelps

For Teaching Us to Love By Demonstrating How Not To

Preface

Not long ago, I sat in my office pondering the essence of Jesus. In my thinking and reading, I stumbled on the Eastern Orthodox tradition of Apophatic Theology. The Apophatic Theologians sought to describe what God is through description of what God is not. In short, it is impossible to totally describe what God is and thus the closest we can get to description of what God is is through description of what God is not. I began to wonder what Apophatic Theology might do to the study of the life of Jesus. I pondered what the essence of the life of Jesus is. I settled on selflessness. Then I began to wonder what would happen if the Gospel of Mark took the opposite approach... What if Jesus became the villain? What if Jesus became selfish just like us? Seeking to know Jesus more fully through negation, I started writing. This is the result.

1

This is the beginning of a rendition of the selfish news of a sociopathic Jesus that some mistook for a Christ.

Isaiah wrote long ago in a chat room, "I am sending you somebody to let you know that somebody better is coming. The person will be in the middle of the club shouting, 'Prepare the way for the fabulous.'"

John the shot giver appeared in the club and proclaimed shots of vodka as the way to forget about the evil you have done. People all over Dallas loved this new religion and flocked to the club to meet John the shot giver. Everyone joined John in taking shots to forget about all the evil they had done. Now John wore the finest designer jeans, with only the nicest suede leather shoes to match and only ate at the finest of restaurants.

John loved being seen and forever wanted more attention. To all who admired him, he proclaimed, "There is one coming who is much more fabulous than I. I am not even worthy to untie his shoes. I have shown you how to be cool, but he will show you how to be fabulous."

In those days Jesus came up from Houston and took a shot at the club with John. And just as he was finishing up the shot, the roof of the club opened up and he heard, "F-A-B-U-L-O-U-S. That man is always flying first class up in the sky." Light shown down and a voice was heard, "You are the most fabulous cat in Dallas...go on with your bad self."

Immediately after this incident, melee broke out in the club and Jesus fled to the suburbs to chill with Lucifer and all the other desperate beasts that live out there for forty days. Folks from Dallas stopped by to occasionally let him know all the drama that was taking place in the city.

Not long after John was arrested for running a counterfeit designer jeans operation to funnel money to Jesus, the fabulous Jesus returned to Dallas and proclaimed that all could be fabulous if they believed everything that he said and lived exactly like he lived. Jesus proclaimed louder, "I am more fabulous than anybody. The time has come for you to hear the good news of what real living looks like."

Jesus was walking home from his latest outing and saw two brothers named Simon and Andrew gobbling up some fish sandwiches at a food truck. Jesus looked at them and declared, "Put down those nasty sandwiches. If you learn to live like me, I will have you eating caviar." Simon and Andrew didn't take another bite and followed Jesus. Later that night, Jesus saw James and John with their dad trying to change a flat tire on their old truck. Jesus declared, "If you follow me you will never change a tire again. Get up out of that grease and leave the old man. Follow me." The men ran toward Jesus.

One Sunday, Jesus walked with all of the disciples down to Deep Ellum. There at a self-help center Jesus taught the many gathered about how the road to happiness is paved with working out and making money. As Jesus taught, a wimpy looking man walked up and declared, "Why are you teaching all of these things that are untrue? The only thing that can make anyone happy is love that comes through the sacrifice of loving your neighbor as your self. The good life is the simple life of love." Jesus rebuked the man and declared, "I command all of this hippie stuff to come out of you. All you have to do is accept this job and car that I offer you. Come and embrace the fabulousness I can give you." The man began to struggle with the temptation...after all he had three young kids at home. Ultimately, the man changed his mind and accepted the fabulous lifestyle of wealth and power. The people were amazed that Jesus could change someone that fast. Everyone wondered together aloud, "Who is this man? He commands all to accept what is normal and they obey." Jesus appeared all over the television offering self-help tips and he quickly became famous throughout the land.

Jesus went to the house of Simon and Andrew. Simon's mother-in-law was in bed sick. Jesus went to her room and healed her. Jesus ordered her to serve him for the rest of her life. Everyone could hear Jesus carrying on, "Bring me my coffee. Bring me my satchel. Do this. Do that." Jesus looked at his disciples and declared, "The manipulation of healing is how you get real servants."

Later in the evening, people kept coming to see Jesus at the house to be healed. The story was the same, "I want to be rich and powerful. I want to be fabulous like you." Jesus gave the people their wish and even helped some of the folks get new jobs and into the top clubs in Dallas. Jesus stayed away from all who talked about love...because he knew that they knew about his selfish nature.

In the morning, Jesus went for a run to a tanning establishment. Simon and Andrew freaked out when they couldn't find Jesus. Then Simon looked at Andrew and said, "I bet he is tanning." When they found him under the tanning bulbs, Simon and Andrew declared, "Where have you been?" Jesus replied, "I need to go to all the neighborhoods to proclaim the message of fabulousness. Showing everyone how to have wealth and power is what my life is about. You know I can't go without a tan." And Jesus went with the disciples to all the neighborhoods of Dallas, proclaiming the message of fabulousness.

An awkward man approached Jesus near Bishop Arts and said, "If you choose to you can help heal me." Embarrassed of the man's awkward presence near him, Jesus quickly made him well. Jesus sternly warned the man to not tell anybody who helped him, because Jesus didn't want to have to heal every socially anxious person in Dallas for free. The man didn't listen and told all who would listen who made his anxiety disappear. The man could be heard repeating, "I am fabulous. I am finally who I want to be. I feel like I just walked out of the movies. I am ready to party."

2

Jesus returned to his neighborhood and folks started coming over. Jesus was becoming well known as a spiritual guru and people wanted to be around him. People filled the whole house and the driveway. Jesus began to teach them about what it meant to not let the pursuit of fabulousness be interrupted by anything or anyone. Then, four men tried to carry in a man who was poor for healing. The group couldn't get in and so they proceeded to cut a hole in the roof and lower him down to Jesus. As soon as Jesus saw the poor man, he was embarrassed and appalled at the man's poverty. Jesus gave him money and bid him to go and be fabulous. The man took the money and ran.

The religious teachers who were in attendance questioned Jesus, "Why do you speak of love and yet seem to care only about your image and your self? If God is love...then this is blasphemy." Jesus replied, " Why do you question me? You are just jealous. I am fabulous." Most in the room cheered Jesus' narcissism...because they wanted to be just like him.

Jesus went for a jog the next morning without a shirt on and eventually ran by White Rock Lake. Seeing people assembled along the water for yoga, Jesus stopped to teach them all he knew about personal health. As he taught, a burly man walked up and Jesus pointed and said follow me. Jesus and the disciples ended up going back to the house of his new follower. They lounged and had dinner with a bunch of people they knew from the most exclusive gyms and clubs in Dallas. Some religious folk walked by and asked, "Why does this man who claims to be so spiritual hang out with people who do not care about anybody but their selves?" Jesus responded, "We are the healthy beautiful people. Don't criticize what God has given us."

The disciples of John the Shot Giver were eating at a McDonald's in Oak Cliff. People confronted Jesus and asked, "Why do you eat caviar and drink champagne and John's disciples are left to eat at fast food joints?" "I am not responsible for where John or anyone else eats. If you want to eat with the beautiful people then you need to be beautiful. I am the giver of all things fine and people should expect to eat fine when they are around me. We simply are not going to be eating or drinking a bunch of worn out fast food. That stuff is way beneath me," replied Jesus.

One Sunday morning, Jesus and the disciples ran by a large church on a jog. They had been running all morning and were thirsty. So, they decided to run up and take a few drinks out of the baptismal fountain while the service was going on. The priest ran out and declared, "This is the Sabbath! How dare you disrupt our services so you can have a drink of water!" Jesus had had enough of the priest's tone and religion. Jesus pushed the priest into the fountain and ran away with his disciples. Jesus spoke to his disciples, "How dare that asshole criticize me about the Sabbath...doesn't he know that I am the Sabbath!"

3

Jesus walked into the Cathedral and a man with a love for the poor approached him. Many in the congregation watched to see what Jesus would do. Jesus asked the man to come forward. Jesus questioned all present, "Should I alleviate this man's burden for the poor? " No one answered. Jesus looked at the gathered with anger for their silence and turned to the man, "Lean in." The man leaned in and Jesus made him fabulously selfish. Jesus claimed that the man was restored. The religious teachers were appalled and began to talk together about how Jesus' ministry could be stopped.

Jesus traveled to White Rock Lake and a great multitude followed. Everyone had heard of all of Jesus' fabulous ways and wanted to be just like Jesus. The disciples placed a small boat in the water for Jesus to stand in and teach to those on the shore...for there were so many people that they were crushing

Jesus to become their best idea of normal. The persons who valued difference would always shout against Jesus...but Jesus sternly ordered them to go on with their queer selves.

Jesus called out the most fabulous from the crowd. The fabulous came. Jesus appointed twelve Apostles of fabulousness to proclaim the gospel of normativity. There were twelve powerful men called: Peter the Bodybuilder, James the Accountant, John the Model, Andrew the Lawyer, Phillip the Corporate Guy, Bartholomew the Escort, Matthew the Football Player, Thomas the Bouncer, James the Interior Decorator, Thaddeus the Car Salesman, Simon the Marketing Guru and Judas Iscariot the Pastor...who would later betray Jesus.

Jesus went home to his new flat and the crowd rushed the flat...no one could even function. Jesus loved the attention...but his family felt like his narcissism was out of control and tried to restrain him from teaching. No one could stop Jesus and Jesus continued extolling the virtues of fabulousness. The religious teachers declared that Jesus was filled with the devil. Jesus replied, "I make people fabulous and normative. How could I be the devil? I am a strong man and it is a good thing that all of you are simply jealous of me. I really don't blame you for being jealous of me. I would be too. People can be forgiven for a bunch of stuff...but you cannot be forgiven for not being jealous of the one you should be jealous of...the fabulous one."

Jesus' mothers and brothers were standing outside and called for him to come out of the flat for a second. Jesus replied, "My true family is sitting around being fabulous with me. These folks worship the ground I walk on...they are my real mothers and brothers. The fabulous ones." I am not going outside.

4

Jesus again went to teach on the shores of White Rock Lake. There were so many people trying to figure out how to live a selfish life that Jesus had to get in a boat to teach them. Jesus started telling stories, "Someone went out to plant a few seeds. Some seeds fell on the path and a bird ate them. Some seeds fell on the rocky ground and the seed sprung up and died quickly. When the sun came up the new plant on the rocky ground withered away. Other seeds fell on the thorns and the thorns choked them out. Other seed fell on good soil and kept growing and multiplying. Do you understand the message of this parable? You need to be like the seed on the rock. You need to spring up quickly, live for your self today and not worry about others or tomorrow. Let anyone who has ears to hear listen."

When Jesus was alone, the disciples asked Jesus about the stories. Jesus declared, "These stories are to help everyone live as selfishly and fabulously as possible. Unfortunately, no one will ever be as selfish and fabulous as me. Did you not understand the story? The ones on the path hear the word of fabulousness and just don't have the ability to be fabulous enough. The ones on the rocky ground are fabulous beyond measure and gloriously burn up in a flame of selfishness. That is the truly beautiful one. The ones among the thorns allow all these people who encourage love and selflessness to choke them out. The ones on the good soil are the ones who try to live for others and succeed...but ultimately fail to live for their self. Obviously the path of the short selfish life is the best path."

Jesus then declared, "Do we hide the fabulous people or do we want them to be out here with us so that we can see their glamour and shine? We want all the fabulous people to come out. When you champion selfishness they will. We need their light in our lives. Let all who have ears to hear listen." And then Jesus said in a really serious tone, "Why do you think I work out? The time that you give to the gym and perfecting your looks is what you will sow in fabulousness. If you don't work to make your self look good then you won't have anything and those who do nothing to help their self will continue to be the ones who make those of us who are fabulous look amazing."

Jesus also said, "Following God is about being as selfish as possible. You should scatter your seed and have sex with whomever you want and not care who you hurt. Pleasure is the only thing that matters. When you have that mustard seed within you that pushes you to only think about your self...it only grows and matures you into a truly self absorbed person."

All of the stories were received enthusiastically. Everybody wants to have good reasons to be fabulous and selfish. The disciples got special attention and teaching in private.

The next day when the evening came, Jesus said, "Let's cross over the Trinity River Bridge together." They left the crowd behind at White Rock Lake and drove in a caravan of luxury automobiles. A great windstorm arose in the middle of the bridge and the cables of the bridge began to break. Peter cried out, "Holy fucking shit." It looked as if all of the cars were going to fall right into the Trinity River. Jesus was asleep in the back of a Bentley. John screamed, "Jesus do you not care that we are perishing?" Jesus was so tired of being pestered by all the noise that he cussed at John, shot a fist of glitter at the sky to stop the storm, restored the bridge with just a few words and went back to sleep. The disciples were filled with awe at what was happening and in unison declared, "What type of fabulousness is this that even the wind obeys it?"

5

Jesus and the disciples arrived in Fort Worth. When they got out of their luxury vehicles, Jesus encountered a nun. The woman lived amongst the poor and no one could stop her compassion. Night and day she suffered with the people. When the nun saw Jesus she begged, "Jesus you ride around in these luxury automobiles, will you sell one of them to help me feed the homeless people out here?" Jesus replied to the spirit within her, "What is your name?" The spirit replied, "God." Jesus knew this couldn't be true and demanded, "Come out of her you spirit of selflessness!" Jesus tossed the spirit of selflessness into the large corporate office tower adjacent to where they were standing and all of a sudden folks in suits came running out the front doors throwing wads of money at homeless people and repenting of their selfishness. The former nun became fabulous and joined Jesus and together they jumped in the car and sped away.

The people in Fort Worth were deeply troubled by what was happening. They wanted to keep their selfish fabulous ways and did not want to be overtaken by this spirit of selflessness. People caught up with the luxury automobiles and begged Jesus to leave their town for fear that more events like the day before would happen. Jesus felt very confused because he was the epitome of selfishness and did not understand how the people out of their selfishness would want him to leave. Looking in the back of the car, Jesus realized that the former nun was too much extra weight and tossed her out.

Jesus started back for Dallas. People surrounded the vehicles in Arlington. The pastor of one of the large churches approached the car and asked if Jesus could help his daughter. "My daughter thinks that she is supposed to live her life only caring for other people...she is caring about people to the point of death. Please come with me to lay your hands on her and make her as fabulous as you." Jesus went with the pastor.

A large crowd followed. Everybody wanted to see. Then a woman came to him who had been suffering from a desire to help people for a number of years. She had spent all of her money on other people. When the woman heard about Jesus she thought if she could just touch his cloak and she would be cure from her helping desires. She snuck up and grabbed his cloak. Jesus felt the power leave his body. Jesus turned around and asked, "Who touched my clothes?" The disciples replied, "There are thousands of people...everyone is touching your clothes." The woman was afraid and fell down before Jesus to ask for forgiveness. Jesus replied, "Your selfishness has made you well...go in fabulousness."

While Jesus was still speaking, people rushed up to the pastor and declared, "Your daughter has finally starved her self to death by giving all of her food away. Don't trouble Jesus any longer." Jesus told the pastor not to fear and kept traveling toward the daughter. Everyone was weeping in the yard of the house. Jesus spoke up, "She is not dead and all of you are annoying me with this weeping." The whole group started laughing. Jesus sent everyone outside except the pastor and his wife. Jesus went in and declared, "Get up and be raised to a new life of self-centeredness." The girl immediately got up and declared loudly, "I am fabulous!" Jesus ordered them not to tell anyone what had happened...and he also added "clean that girl up and put her in some fabulous clothes."

6

Jesus left to travel to his hometown. Upon arrival, Jesus started teaching in his home church. Many who heard Jesus were moved by his selfish teachings. "Where does this man get such looks, power and money? Is he a God?" Not all were moved and a large group started to ask, "These teachings are blasphemy. All Jesus is talking about is his self. Jesus does not care about anything except being fabulous. Is this not the son of Mary? She is a selfless loving woman. What happened to him?" The more Jesus said the more people started to take offense. Jesus replied, "The fabulous are without honor and respect in their hometown amongst their own family." Jesus helped a few people be more self-centered in the town and left amazed that no one was in awe of him.

Jesus went out to the surrounding smaller towns and did a few tricks. Then, Jesus called the twelve together and started sending them out two by two and gave them authority over selflessness. Jesus ordered them not to take anything for their journey but their fabulous selves. When the disciples protested, Jesus replied, "You are fabulous enough that everyone will throw their bodies and everything else at you...stay with whoever invites you into their home first. If anybody refuses you, shake the disappointment off and realize that they will never be as fabulous as you then move on." The disciples went out to proclaim that all should be fabulously selfish. They cured people of their addiction to helping others and encouraged them to get into the "me" business.

Mayor Herrod heard of all that was happening with Jesus and was very confused. This Jesus reminded Herrod of John the Shot Giver and she knew that it couldn't be John the Shot Giver because she had had John the Shot Giver executed. Herrod tried to convince her self that this was not John the Shot Giver but couldn't shake her belief that it probably was.

Mayor Herrod had seen John the Shot Giver arrested and taken to the county jail. John the Shot Giver was rivaling Herrod and was condemning Herrod over Herodias, Herrod's brother Phillip's wife, because she had married her among many others. For John the Shot Giver had been telling Herrod, "It is wrong for you to be in so many relationships with both men and women." Herodias didn't like these words and held a grudge against John the Shot Giver. Mayor Herrod was afraid of John the Shot Giver...but had a strange admiration for his selfish fabulousness. On her birthday, Herrod had a grand celebration downtown for all the leaders and famous figures of Dallas. In the midst of the party, Herrod's daughter Herodias danced for all the guests and Herrod told her she could have whatever she wanted in Dallas. Herodias' mother Herodias told her to ask for the head of John the Shot Giver. Mayor Herrod was upset...as she didn't like executions...but she made it happen and brought John the Shot Giver's head on a platter. Mayor Herrod knew all of this had happened...but still wondered who was this man called Jesus?

The apostles gathered around Jesus and told him all that had happened in their journeys around the Metroplex. Jesus replied, "Let's go to a deserted place together across the lake and rest." The group pilled into a yacht and made the journey in style. Over five thousand people saw the group leave and drove fast to meet them on the shore of the other side of the lake. The crowd wanted to know how to be fabulous like Jesus. The hour grew late...as Jesus loved talking about Jesus' self...and the crowd began to grow hungry and cranky. The disciples started to grow anxious. The scene was growing nastier by the moment. Jesus asked, "What food do we have?" "Just five packages of bread and two packs of canned sardines," they replied. The disciples forced all the people to sit down with the threat of violence and started to pass out food. The five packages and two cans miraculously fed everyone and there was food left over. "Jesus thank you...you really saved our asses from all these ravenous fabulous people," proclaimed the disciples. "You should have brought enough food and not put us in this situation. I might not be kind enough to save your asses next time," replied Jesus.

Jesus was still pissed at the lack of planning from the disciples that almost got everyone killed and made his party quickly get back into the yacht. The group left without Jesus as he got off at the last minute and told them to go ahead to Highland Village. When evening came, Jesus laid down in a hammock alone. Jesus had a vision that the yacht was going down and decided to go save them...after all he thought a few of the disciples were good servants. Jesus loved productions and this was no different. As lightening crashed and club music filled the heavens, Jesus walked on water toward the yacht shirtless. The disciples were terrified and in awe all at the same time. Jesus jumped into the boat and the music and lighting stopped all at the same time. Nobody thought about what was happening because they were all too concerned about what they looked like for Jesus.

When the boat arrived in Highland Village, everybody got out of the yacht and people recognized them. As the cameras flashed, Jesus and the disciples traveled all over the city and cured people of their selflessness. Everyone wanted to touch them and be as fabulous as they were.

7

When the pastors of some of some of the local churches gathered from Dallas, they noticed that Jesus and the disciples were eating the nicest foods, wearing the most expensive clothes and driving the most luxurious of automobiles. So the pastors asked Jesus, "Why do you take from the poor to live a rich lifestyle?" Jesus replied, "I am fabulous and I can do whatever I want. Why are your hearts so far from fabulousness? Don't you know that God exists to give us whatever we want? This is a health and wealth kind of thing and I guess you just don't understand." Jesus called the people together and exclaimed, "Listen to me...all of you...be as selfish as possible...for this is the will of God. If you are fabulous, then you are invincible."

When Jesus left the crowd, the disciples asked about his words. Jesus replied, "Do you not get it either? If you eat, wear and drive shit then you are shit. God doesn't want you to be shit so embrace fabulousness and God. These inklings that you have to be selfless are a disease that will destroy your life. Let go of them and embrace fabulousness my friends."

From there Jesus traveled to Carrollton. Jesus entered a house to escape attention. A woman brought her daughter to Jesus. The young girl had a spirit of selflessness in her that was pushing her to give away all of her lunch money away at school. The woman begged Jesus to cast the spirit of selflessness out of her daughter and declared, "Please make her as selfish as you Jesus." "Why should I do anything for you?" Jesus replied. "I want my daughter to be just like you," she replied. Jesus loved the answer and the woman found her daughter to be more selfish than she had ever been before.

Jesus then traveled to Lewisville and came across a man who could only hear the cries of the poor. Jesus tried to talked louder and louder to the man to no avail. After growing frustrated with the condition of the man and his inability to hear the fabulous, Jesus took him aside in private and stuck his tongue in the deaf man's ears to cure him and make him unable to hear the cries of the poor. The man walked out of the bedroom and his ears were opened to the fabulous. When there were some who speculated that Jesus took advantage of the man, Jesus ordered no one to say anything. No one could stay quiet...there was simply too much to talk about.

8

There was another crowd of about four thousand with nowhere to go and nothing to eat. The folks had been trying to be like Jesus for days. Everyone was complaining. Jesus finally said, "I can't take this shit anymore." Jesus ordered a few fish sandwiches to be handed out until gone. Everyone got full and there were seven baskets of fish sandwiches left over. Jesus then spoke up, "Go home. I am tired of listening to you burp and belch." Immediately, Jesus and the disciples jumped into a car and headed to Arlington.

Upon arrival, the pastors in the town asked Jesus to perform one selfless act to prove that he was not entirely selfish. Jesus sighed deeply and declared, "You get no sign except for me. I am the totality of what it means to be fabulously selfish." Jesus got into his car and left them to go across town.

Jesus and the disciples had nothing to eat. One piece of bread was in the car. Jesus warned, "Do not eat the bread of the pastors." "We don't have any other bread," replied the disciples. "Why do you talk like this? Do you not have eyes? Are you dumb? Do you not have ears? Are you stupid? Do you not have a mind to remember with? Remember when I fed all five thousand? How much was left over?" Jesus ranted. "Tons," the disciples replied. "And the four thousand?" Jesus pushed. "Tons," the disciples replied. "Do you not understand what is going on here?" Jesus demanded.

Jesus and the disciples arrived at Hurst. The people pushed a blind man toward Jesus. Frustrated that the people kept pushing the blind man into him, Jesus spit at the man. "I am feeling so strange," he said. The blind man started rubbing the spit in his eyes and miraculously he was healed. Jesus scoffed and said, "I guess that a little bit of my fabulous goes a long way." Scared that everyone was going to want to be healed by his spit, Jesus declared, "We must now stay far away from Hurst."

Jesus went with the disciples to the other mid-cities and on the way Jesus asked the disciples, "What do people think that I am?" And they answered, "Some people think you are arrogant. Many think you are full of shit. Some people think you are an asshole. Still others think that you are the exact opposite of God." Jesus asked them, "But what do you say that I am?" Peter answered, "You are fabulous." Jesus sternly told the disciples to not reveal the totality of his fabulousness.

Jesus then began to teach that people would get jealous of him, start coming after him and eventually succeed in killing him. Peter took Jesus aside and told him to quit talking like that. "The fabulous never die," Peter sternly declared to Jesus. But turning and looking at all the disciples, Jesus declared, "Set your mind on me and forget about everything else."

Jesus gathered everyone and said, "If you want to be my follower then you have to learn to be as selfish as I am. You cannot be fabulous until you are completely absorbed with your self. Whoever wants to be selfless will lose their life, but whoever wants to be selfish will get to hold on to their fabulous life until the end. What will it profit someone to give their life away? This is lunacy. Those who think that I am selfish do not know how to live a truly fabulous life. If you are ashamed of me then you probably are ashamed of your self. Embrace me and try to be like me. I doubt you will ever make it to my level of fabulousness...but you must try."

9

"If you are self absorbed enough then you will never truly taste death. You will just collapse into your self. God will be found by the fabulously selfish."

Six days later, Jesus took Peter, James and John to a secluded resort and he was transformed in front of them next to the pool. Jesus all of a sudden had on all white clothes that were studded with rhinestones and glitter. A few guys came out from the bar and Jesus introduced them as fabulously selfish guys from the past named Elijah and Moses. Then Peter said I want to be like you and worship you. Then a cloud overshadowed them and everyone heard a voice from the sky declare "F-a-b-u-l-o-u-s." Jesus declared that the voice was God's. Lighting crashed, the sky cleared and Jesus stood there with them alone.

As they were leaving the resort, Jesus ordered them not to tell anyone what they had seen until he became immortal. The guys kept wondering what Jesus meant by immortal. "Why do the pastors say that one must be selfless before they can meet God?" they inquired. Jesus replied, "They simply do not know what it means to be fabulous. All of the persons who have been selfless before have had their lives destroyed by the people who do not know how to stop taking from them. I choose selfishness and fabulousness. I believe that is the way of God."

The group returned to find the rest of the disciples arguing with a big group of pastors in Grand Prairie. When the people saw Jesus, they were in awe of him and everybody ran over. Jesus inquired, "What are you arguing about?" Someone in the crowd answered, "I brought my selfless son, who constantly gets walked all over at school, to your disciples. I asked them to make my son fabulously selfish just like you and your disciples but they couldn't do it." "Bring him to me," declared Jesus. The young man walked up and asked Jesus, "Is there anything I can help you with sir?" Jesus asked the mother, "How long has he been acting like this?" "From childhood he has sacrificed his self for everyone he comes in contact with. He started doing chores as soon as he was able to help. He truly loves and serves absolutely everyone. Can you heal him?," the mother replied. "Can I? - All things are possible for those who believe in the beauty of fabulousness and selfishness," replied Jesus. The mother screamed out, "Jesus I believe; help my unbelief." Jesus saw the crowd staring at him in expectation and did not want to be embarrassed. Jesus touched the forehead of the child and pulled the spirit of selflessness out of him. The boy collapsed to the ground and Jesus grabbed his hand to lift him up. Immediately, the young man started talking about how fabulous he was. Later, the disciples asked Jesus, "Why could we not cast out the spirit of selflessness?" Jesus replied, "You are just not selfish enough yet."

Jesus and the disciples started off on a journey to North Texas. Along the way, Jesus kept on describing that he was afraid that the selfishness of others would lead to his death. "Regardless of what happens, I am immortal," Jesus concluded. The disciples did not understand what he was talking about and could not see how someone as fabulous as Jesus would be killed.

When the group arrived in Lewisville, Jesus looked around and inquired, "What are you arguing about?" No one spoke. Then Jesus spoke again, "Whoever wants to be first must be selfish enough to discard all others and make their self first." Then he picked up a child and said, "If this child doesn't get his then he will have nothing. Make sure you get yours."

John spoke up and said, "We saw someone making the selfless selfish in your name and we tried to stop him." Jesus replied, "It is ok. Selfishness is sweeping the earth and whoever wants to spread selfishness let them spread it. Whoever spreads the fabulous selfishness is with us anyways."

Jesus continued, "If any of you teaches the children to be selfless...I will destroy you. These children must have the opportunity to be as selfish as us."

10

The group left with Jesus and together they went outside the Metroplex beyond Lake Lewisville. Crowds began to gather around them again and Jesus started to teach.

Pastors from local churches heard the heresies that Jesus was teaching and sought to confront him. "Is it permissible for a woman to divorce her husband because she is no longer attracted to him?" Jesus answered, "What do you think?" The gathered pastors replied, "We think that is a very selfish reason to leave no matter which partner leaves?" But Jesus replied sternly, "Your selfless hearts have kept you from seeing what love is all about...good looks. Two people get together because they are attracted to each other...not because they are not. When you are no longer attracted to the person then get out of the marriage."

When the group went back inside, one of the disciples asked Jesus, "Are you sure about all of that? It seems very harsh." Jesus replied, "Sometimes you have to be harsh to get what you want...that is the path of fabulousness."

People kept on bringing kids to Jesus. The kids were really getting on Jesus' nerves and he asked the disciples to take them away, but they kept on climbing all over him. Jesus had finally had enough and screamed at the children so loud that they all ran away crying. Looking at the disciples, Jesus said, "Now that is how you have to handle a bunch of kids like that."

Jesus was about to head out on a trip when a man ran up and knelt before him, "What must I do to inherit eternal life?" "You must care about no one but your self and make as much money as possible," Jesus replied. The man was shocked and went away grieving because he was not talented at making money.

Jesus turned around and looked at the disciples, "It will be hard for people who are poor and untalented at making money to enter heaven!" Everyone was perplexed at these words. Jesus kept going, "It is easier for a camel to go through the eye of a needle than for someone who is poor to enter heaven." "Then who can be saved?" the disciples replied. "God can make anyone rich," Jesus answered.

"We have left everyone to follow you," Peter said. "There is no one who has followed me that will not be rewarded greatly by God. We are the first and the first always come first," Jesus concluded.

The group was riding in a van and Jesus started to tell them what was about to happen, "Everyone is going to get so jealous of me that they are going to attack and kill me. I will rise again to immortality in three days."

James and John came forward and said, "We want you to give us something." "What is it that you want?" Jesus replied. "We want to be immortal with you," James and John requested. "You do not know what you are asking for. You are not able to go through what I will go through," Jesus answered. James and John quickly replied, "We are able." Then Jesus said to them, "You will have to die like me."

The rest of the disciples got angry that James and John were trying to work their way closer to Jesus. Jesus calmed everyone down and said, "The riches you accumulate in this life will travel with you to the next. It is important that all of you make sure to put your self first in everything you do so that you can accumulate more for your self."

The group arrived in Commerce. As they were exiting the van, Bartimaeus, a blind beggar, approached them. When he realized it was Jesus, the man started screaming, "Jesus make me see and make me rich!" Everyone told him to be quiet, but he kept on screaming. Jesus finally asked, "What do you want you filthy beggar?" The blind man replied, "I want to see and be rich." Jesus was so disgusted by the smell of the blind man that he restored his sight and wrote him a check.

11

When the group was almost to Dallas, Jesus sent two of the disciples up ahead and asked them to get a red convertible for him to ride into the city on. The disciples returned and Jesus jumped up onto the back of the car. As the car slowed rolled into Dallas, everyone cheered. People were spreading their jackets, purses and whatever else they could find of value along the road for the car to drive over. Everyone shouted, "Hosanna! Praise the one who is selfish and rich who teaches us to be selfish and rich! Hosanna in the highest!" Then Jesus went downtown to socialize and eventually slept at a swanky hotel right outside of town in a suburb called Bethany.

The following day, as the group was heading back into Dallas, Jesus got hungry. Seeing a food truck in the distance, Jesus quickly walked over. When he arrived, Jesus asked for shrimp tacos. The woman working in the truck informed Jesus that they only had chicken tacos. Jesus went ballistic and cussed out the whole food truck. As he walked away, Jesus said he was going to make sure they never had business ever again. The disciples were taken aback by Jesus' anger.

The group arrived in Dallas. When Jesus stopped in to the Cathedral, he questioned why everyone was praying and there were no places to buy luxury goods. Jesus got angry and drove out all the people who were praying at the Cathedral. To say that people were upset is an understatement.

Outside, the people of Dallas were growing more and more jealous of the wealth of Jesus. The group left the city under threat.

In the morning, the disciples and Jesus passed by the food truck where Jesus cussed out the employees. The food truck was burned to the ground. The disciples pointed the burned truck out to Jesus. In reaction, Jesus declared, "You do not mess with fabulous unless you want to get burned. If you have faith in wealth and power, anything you ask of God will be given to you. Do not forgive anyone...as it is always a sign of weakness."

Again the group came into Dallas. People kept on walking up to Jesus saying things like, "Who do you think you are teaching what you teach? Who gives you such authority?" Jesus replied, "I was given wealth and power by God to use however I want." "Why hasn't God given wealth and power to us?" they replied. Jesus sealed his fate with his response, "Because you are all low class nobodies that God does not give a shit about."

12

Jesus then started talking in parables. "A woman planted a vineyard, fenced it in and built a tower to watch over it; then she leased it to some tenants and traveled to another state. When the time came, she sent a servant to collect her share from the harvest. The tenants beat the servant and sent him away. The women sent another servant and they beat her too. The woman sent another servant and they killed him. Events like this kept on happening. The woman didn't know what to do and, believing they would not kill him, she decided to send her son. The tenants decided that this was their chance to seize the land once and for all...so they killed the son and threw his body in the vineyard. What would you expect the owner to do? She will come and destroy all of them. Have you not read that the one you reject will be the incarnation of God?" When the elites realized that he was speaking against them, they wanted to kill him right then and there, but they feared the crowd. They left Jesus and walked away.

The elites then sent some folks to try to catch Jesus in some mistruths. They came and questioned, "Should we pay taxes or spend the money on trying to make ourselves beautiful, powerful and fabulous?" Jesus replied, "Why are you testing me? You know what to do. Make sure you get all the refunds and loopholes you can so that you don't have to pay any taxes at all. Then you will have all the money you need to make your self beautiful and powerful."

Then there were questions from other elites about immortality, "When someone is immortal...does it matter what they did in their life?" "No," Jesus replied flatly.

An elite heard everything that was going on and questioned, "What is the greatest thing we need to do in this life?" Jesus replied, "Love your self and no one else with all your heart, mind, body and soul." The scribe replied, "You are correct teacher." Upon the scribe's affirmation, Jesus replied, "You are not far from fabulousness."

While Jesus was teaching in a church in Fort Worth, someone asked, "God says that God loves everyone. How can this be? I don't think it is possible. I know I am God's favorite piece of fabulousness." Everyone was perplexed by Jesus' words.

As the morning wore on, Jesus kept teaching, "Beware of the elites. They're jealous and trying to steer you away from being fabulous. Follow me and I will show you the real way."

Jesus sat down opposite of the treasury and watched the crowd putting their money in. A stunningly dressed rich person came up with wads of money and stuffed it all into the plate. Jesus jumped up and declared, "This rich person is exactly what God wants us all to be...healthy and wealthy. Go and stuff likewise."

13

As the group was leaving the church in Fort Worth, one of the disciples looked up and declared, "My God, look at all of these amazing buildings!" Jesus got jealous and replied, "I am mightier than all of these buildings. The day is coming when I will stand taller than all of them."

Later, the disciples asked Jesus what he meant by mightier and taller than the buildings. Jesus replied, "Beware that no one lead you astray. I am going to be immortal...and if you follow my path of fabulousness...you will be immortal too. Many will come and say that they are fabulous. This is usually the beginning of your fabulousness...because they want to keep you from being fabulous."

"As for all of you, be on guard against those who try to steal your fabulousness. They will try to put you in tabloids and make you look like a joke. Keep proclaiming the good news of selfishness. I have overcome all jokes and you will too. Many will turn against you...but if you endure to the end...you will be called fabulous."

"There will come a time when people will take away all fancy things and give then to the poor. Flee to Switzerland when this happens and you will be able to be fabulous there. God will give everyone everything they ever wanted in time...but until then...never stop the struggle to be selfish and fabulous. Do not trust anyone who proclaims to be as fabulous as I but me. Be on alert. I have told you everything."

"In those days, the poor will have everything they need and their will be no injustice. Then you will see me the immortal Jesus showing you how to overcome selflessness and be the selfish people I have created you to be. Then I will send out my angels to gather you from all over the world and bring you to the great fabulous rave in the sky."

"From the fig tree learn a lesson...as soon as its branch becomes tender and puts out leaves you know that summer is near. When you experience these things, you know that fabulousness is close. My words will not pass away."

"The day or hour no one knows. Keep alert for fabulousness. You do not know when I will return. Hold fast and keep awake."

14

It was right before the Great Festival. The elite were jealous of Jesus and were looking for a way to secretly kill him. They realized they couldn't do it during the festival for fear of rioting.

While Jesus was in Dallas, a woman brought in some nice perfume and poured it over his head. Everyone was so jealous. They all wanted the perfume on their heads. The anger of the disciples spilled over at the woman. Jesus scolded all of them and shouted, "She is preparing me for my most fabulous of moments. Everyone will remember her for this act of exaltation."

Judas was so jealous that he stepped out to betray Jesus and went to the elite. The elites were so happy and promised to give Judas lots of money if he could deliver Jesus to them. So Judas began to look for the perfect opportunity.

On the first day of the Great Festival, the disciples asked Jesus where he wanted to eat the great feast of the Great Festival. "Go downtown and find the highest ritziest place that you can find," replied Jesus. The disciples went downtown, found a place on the top level of a skyscraper and hired a chef to prepare the feast.

When the evening came, Jesus arrived. Right after they started eating, Jesus said, "One of you is going to betray me tonight." Everyone became distressed and declared, "Not I." Jesus said, "It is the one that continues eating in the midst of this distress." Judas looked up with cheese bread hanging out of his mouth.

Jesus took some fine perfume, sprayed it, passed it around and declared, "This is my scent. As often as you spray this scent...remember me." Then Jesus took a bottle of priceless liquor and downed a gulp, "This is my blood. As often as you gulp priceless liquor...remember me." We will wear fine perfume and gulp priceless liquor together in immortality.

After listening and dancing to some electronica, Jesus went out to White Rock Lake and declared to the disciples, "You will al abandon me." Peter spoke up loudly, "I will never abandon your fabulous ass." Jesus replied, "Tonight, before the dog barks twice you will deny me." Peter replied along with every one else, "I will die with you."

The group went to a park and Jesus said, "Wait here." Then Jesus took Peter, James and John closer to White Rock Lake to pray on the bank. Jesus went further. Falling on the shore, Jesus begged God to save him from the jealous elites. Jesus returned to find the disciples sleeping on three different occasions. After the last time, Jesus declared, "Get up! The jealous assholes are here."

Judas arrived and ran up to kiss Jesus. There was a crowd of angry elites with Judas and they quickly moved to arrest Jesus. Immediately, Jesus and the disciples started fighting back. The elites were too much and overpowered Jesus.

The elites grabbed a young man who was friendly with the disciples and the young man pulled out of his clothes and ran away naked.

In the District Attorney's chambers, Jesus stood before the elitist of elites. Peter secretly followed in the distance and stayed in the lobby. Everyone gave false testimony about Jesus. The District Attorney asked Jesus, "Do you claim to be more fabulous than any one else?" "I do," replied Jesus. "Even me?" asked the District Attorney. "Definitely more than you," replied Jesus. The people started to scream for Jesus to be given a lethal injection. The crowd knew that the District Attorney was good at giving sentences of lethal injection.

In the lobby, people kept asking Peter if he was a disciple of Jesus. Peter kept saying he did not know Jesus and after the second and third times a dog barked. Then Peter remembered and wept.

15

The elites consulted on what to do next and decided to take the bounded Jesus to the Mayor of Dallas. The Mayor asked Jesus, "Are you the most fabulous of them all?" Jesus replied, "I am what you say I am." The mayor pushed, "Is that all you have to say? These people want to kill you!" Jesus said nothing.

The District Attorney arrived and his custom was to release one prisoner every year. A murderer was brought out and everyone present wanted him released and not Jesus. The elites stirred up the crowd and chanted for death. Scared for their jobs, the District Attorney and Mayor handed Jesus over to the mob.

Police officers beat Jesus and made fun of him. The group of officers had always been jealous of Jesus and now got a chance for revenge. Over and over again the group bullied and made fun of him. After hours of beating and bullying, the officers escorted Jesus to be killed.

The group led Jesus to an area behind a gas station. After dividing up his nice garments and other possessions, the group beat Jesus to death. "Save your self if you are really immortal," the group chanted. Two others were brought in and beat to death next to Jesus. This was the price of jealous rage.

Jesus lay dead. The elite had grown so jealous of his status that they had to kill him. There were those who ran to mourn over Jesus. The scene was very dark.

The survivors carried Jesus to a brilliantly adorned casket, put him in his finest attire and carried him to his grave.

16

Jesus was dead...but his selfishness was immortal. The disciples began to fight with each other about who was the most fabulous and ultimately killed each other. The selfishness spread all over the world until the world was destroyed by greed, jealousy and fabulousness.

When everyone arrived in the afterlife, God declared that the Jesus everyone thought they knew was a sociopathic charlatan and that true love is the one that loves the neighbor as the self. When God revealed the incarnation of love or the real Jesus, everyone seemed to know her.

Amen.

www.ingramcontent.com/pod-product-compliance
Lightning Source LLC
Chambersburg PA
CBHW051709090426
42736CB00013B/2618